JANUARY 50 COLORING PAGES
FOR ADULTS RELAXATION

SHIH CHIEN HUA

PUBLISHED BY:
SHIH CHIEN HUA
Copyright © 2018

SEABIRD SHOP >50FOR

FB FAN PAGE

Disclaimer
The information contained in this book is for general information purposes only. The information is provided by the authors and while we endeavor to keep the information up to date and correct, we make no representations or warranties of any kind, express or implied, about the completeness, accuracy, reliability, suitability or availability with respect to the book or the information, products, services, or related graphics contained in the book for any purpose. Any reliance you place on such information is therefore strictly at your own risk.

JANUARY 1ST

note:

_____

_____

_____

JANUARY 2ND

note:

_____

_____

_____

JANUARY 3RD

note:

_____

_____

_____

JANUARY 4TH

note:

_____

_____

_____

JANUARY 5TH

note:

_____

_____

_____

JANUARY 6TH

note:

_____

_____

_____

JANUARY 7TH

note:

_____

_____

_____

JANUARY 8TH

note:

_____

_____

_____

JANUARY 9TH

note:

_____

_____

_____

JANUARY 10TH

note:

_____

_____

_____

JANUARY 11TH

note:

_____

_____

_____

JANUARY 12TH

note:

_____

_____

_____

JANUARY 15TH

note:

_____

_____

_____

JANUARY 14TH

note:

_____

_____

_____

JANUARY 15TH

note:

_____

_____

_____

JANUARY 16TH

note:

_____

_____

_____

JANUARY 17TH

note:

_____

_____

_____

JANUARY 18TH

note:

_____

_____

_____

JANUARY 19TH

note:

_____

_____

_____

JANUARY 20TH

note:

_____

_____

_____

JANUARY 21TH

note:

_____

_____

_____

JANUARY 22TH

note:

_____

_____

_____

JANUARY 25TH

note:

_____

_____

_____

JANUARY 24TH

note:

_____

_____

_____

JANUARY 25TH

note:

_____

_____

_____

JANUARY 26TH

note:

_____

_____

_____

JANUARY 27TH

note:

_____

_____

_____

JANUARY 28TH

note:

_____

_____

_____

JANUARY 29TH

note:

_____

_____

_____

JANUARY 30TH

note:

_____

_____

_____

JANUARY 31TH

note:

_____

_____

_____

JANUARY 32TH

note:

_____

_____

_____

JANUARY 35TH

note:

_____

_____

_____

JANUARY 34TH

note:

_____

_____

_____

JANUARY 35TH

note:

_____

_____

_____

JANUARY 36TH

note:

_____

_____

_____

JANUARY 37TH

note:

_____

_____

_____

JANUARY 30TH

note:

_____

_____

_____

JANUARY 39TH

note:

_____

_____

_____

JANUARY 40TH

note:

_____

_____

_____

JANUARY 41TH

note:

_____

_____

_____

JANUARY 42TH

note:

_____

_____

_____

JANUARY 45TH

note:

_____

_____

_____

JANUARY 44TH

note:

_____

_____

_____

JANUARY 45TH

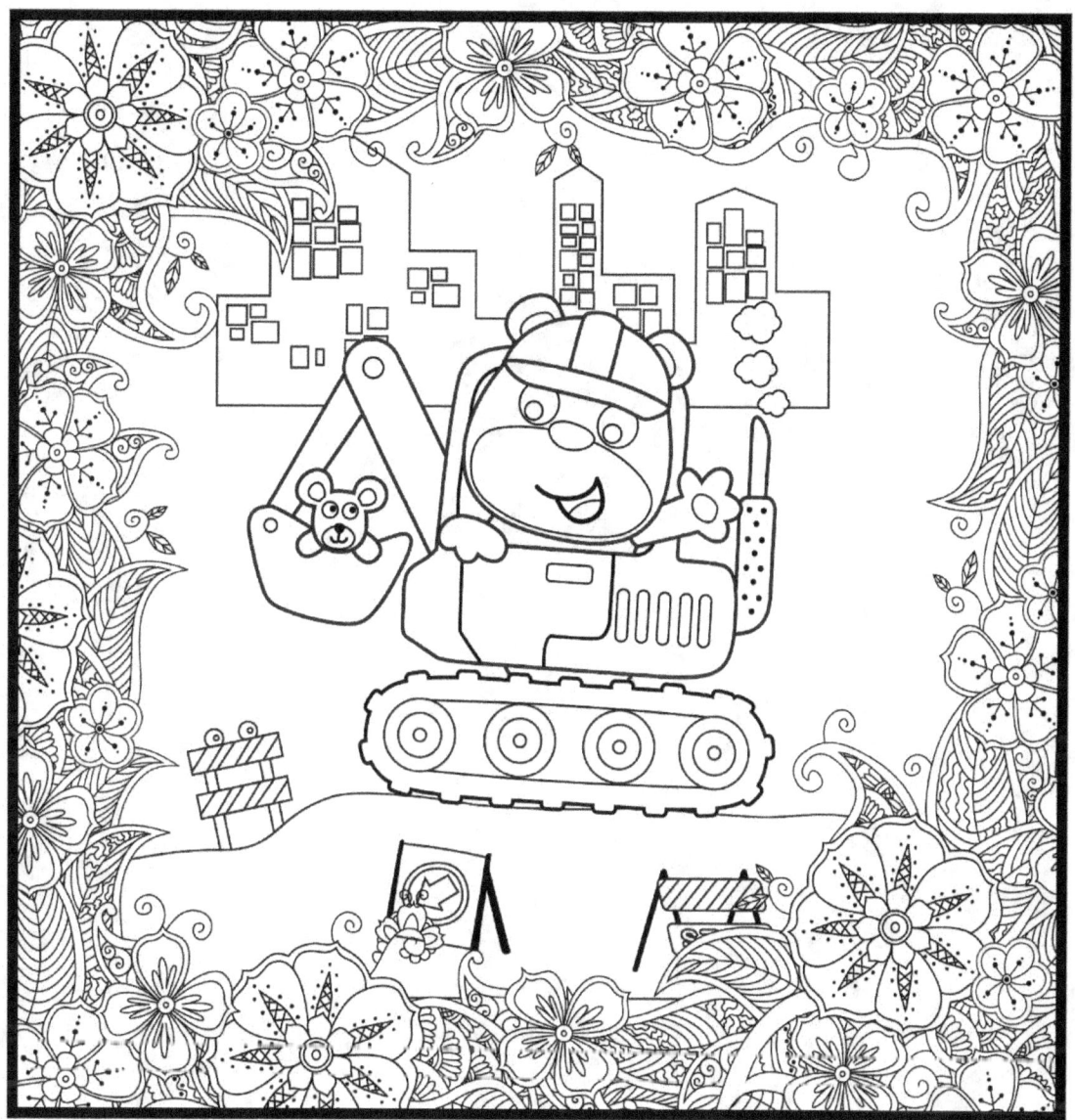

note:

_____

_____

_____

JANUARY 46TH

note:

_____

_____

_____

JANUARY 47TH

note:

_____

_____

_____

JANUARY 48TH

note:

_____

_____

_____

JANUARY 49TH

note:

_____

_____

_____

JANUARY 50TH

note:

_____

_____

_____